YOU KNOW YOU'RE 60 WHEN . . .

ALSO BY RICHARD SMITH

THE DIETER'S GUIDE TO WEIGHT LOSS DURING SEX

THE BRONX DIET

NEWLYWEDS' GUIDE TO SEX ON THE FIRST NIGHT

101 USES FOR AN EX-HUSBAND

RICHARD SMITH'S GUIDE TO GETTING EVEN

YOU KNOW YOU'RE 50 WHEN . . .

THE KITTY KAMA SUTRA

YOUR CAT'S JUST NOT THAT INTO YOU

EVERYTHING I NEED TO KNOW I LEARNED FROM MY DOG

LOVE MUSCLE OF DURANGO

Richard Smith

Illustrated by Debra J. Solomon

BROADWAY BOOKS • NEW YORK

Published in the United States by Broadway Books, an imprint of the Crown Publishing Group, a division of Random House, Inc., New York.
www.crownpublishing.com

Library of Congress Cataloging-in-Publication Data
is available upon request.

ISBN 978-0-307-58762-6

Printed in the United States of America

Design by Jennifer Ann Daddio/Bookmark Design & Media Inc.

1 3 5 7 9 10 8 6 4 2

First Edition

To cigars, single malt scotch, and superior genes . . .
may they keep me from ever needing a hip replacement

INTRODUCTION

"Never have wild sex with anyone who doesn't know CPR."

—HEALTH CARE SPECIALIST WHO PREFERS ANONYMITY

Despite the many books purporting to help us not just experience, but actually take pleasure in, finally becoming adults, few guidelines exist for those who find themselves underqualified for the job of turning 60. Inside you feel 30 or 40, but you are now urged to get a colonoscopy. Or you're suddenly plagued by age-related doubts: Which country is my bedsore shaped like? What about pasta buildup in my aorta? Should I fund my daughter's Ph.D. or have my teeth whitened? Am I a terrible person because I still never get up at night to pee? I'm dating a man half my age—should I tell my husband? Is there a secret to feeling less suicidal when trying to understand my drug plan?

In other words, why be a slave to your birth certificate? Inside you know you're only 42, or 27, or, if you're addicted to hard living, 96. Act the age you think you should be while asking yourself: Should I flatten anyone who refers to me as a Golden Ager? Can these knees support another marathon?

You not only want to fight aging, you want to frighten it. These pages will help.

Note: The guidelines in this book have not been reviewed by the FDA.

YOU KNOW YOU'RE 60 WHEN . . .

DOCTOR: I have some good news and some bad news.

PATIENT: What's the bad news?

DOCTOR: You've got cancer.

PATIENT: What's the good news?

DOCTOR: You won't outlive your money.

DID YOU KNOW.

AT THE DOCTOR'S OFFICE, YOUR CO-PAY IS EXCUSED IF:

1. All the good magazines are taken.

2. The person on your left with the hacking cough refuses to cover his mouth.

- The first thing you look at in the newspaper is the obituaries.

- Happiness is a heating pad.

- You realize there's a causal connection between clipping coupons and premature aging.

- Super-hold hair gel still doesn't make you look like an indie rock star.

- You've attended the funerals of your two favorite cardiologists.

- You agonize over how to diplomatically tell the home care worker not to look in your purse.

- Your children never call because they still live with you.

- Aerobic activity includes drooling.

- Before going out, you stand before a mirror wondering, *Can these boobs still hold up this clingy little top?* (. . . as you reach for the underwire).

- You fill the gap between breakfast and the early-bird special with free samples at the mall.

- You're becoming increasingly fluent in doctor and medspeak (for example: ischemia).

- At gatherings, you secretly compare your liver spots to others'.

- You raise cash for a brow lift by selling your signed Beatles poster on eBay.

- You have no problem lying about your age. (Why be a slave to your birth certificate?)

- When it's cold and damp outside, you begin to mildew.

- Your mail includes certain items that arrive in discreet, tamper-evident packages.

- The grinning white-haired couple in magazine ads that read "We're having so much fun" disgusts you.

- The only high you still get is from standing up too quickly.

- The special things you have in common with your new lover are bingo and arthritis.

- Hints from your parents to get a place of your own become less subtle.

- When stepping onto an escalator, you hesitate until you get the "good" tread.

- You realize life is getting shorter and spring for the BMW you've always wanted.

- The defiant part of you vows to continue to eat the foods that don't agree with you, until they've learned their lesson.

- Your knees are begging to be replaced.

NEW YEAR'S RESOLUTIONS—I WILL:

Lead a more dissolute life. (Just once, I want to hear someone in law enforcement say, "Come out with your hands up.")

Decide what I want to be when I grow up.

Lie about my age without guilt.

Embrace positive vibes: edit out all the bad stuff in my diaries.

Discover the meaning of life.

Engage in at least five age-defying activities:

Run a marathon.

Eat more saturated fat.

Have the courage to ask a friend how old I really look.

Explore off-label uses of scotch (like spiking my morning cocoa and chilling when my in-laws stop by).

Beat those afternoon blahs through high-quality naps.

Get a dueling scar.

Take a road trip in a stolen car.

Improve my nutrition—attend only gallery openings where they serve organic wine and cheese.

Stop saying "Oy!" from the effort of opening an umbrella.

Put my cardiologist on speed dial. I will call him twice daily and hold the phone to my chest so he can hear how nicely my heart is beating.

Do good deeds.

Help a weary Boy Scout cross the street.

Save a life by telling an elderly customer in the supermarket that he's about to buy milk that's past its expiration date.

Talk a candy striper into giving me a happy ending.

Avoid the sun—that's why I have a gardener.

Be more proactive and learn to direct the conversation back to my triple bypass. I rule!

Do serious harm to any well-meaning driver who kneels the bus for me.

Buy a treadmill and assess the health of the new man in my life by putting him on it.

Learn CPR, just in case. Practice on a veal roast.

- From a late-night infomercial, you secretly order a product that keeps hair from growing out of your ears.
- Your Rolodex contains several potential organ donors in case you have to call in a favor.
- You part your hair in the middle and no one notices.
- You harness restless leg syndrome to power a rocker.
- You supplement your Social Security by selling your expired drugs on eBay.
- Your Facebook profile includes your medical history.
- The successful descent of a steep flight of stairs becomes a media event.
- Gray is the new blond.
- WebMD is your home page.

- You turn a scary color while trying to blow out the 61 candles on your birthday cake.

- Your life coach dies.

DO
It
NOW!
GO
GO
GO

TERMS USED THROUGHOUT THIS BOOK

Senior Inertia Medical term defined as a reluctance to move one's body once it has made contact with a soft surface such as a sofa, favorite armchair, or cat.

"&#^&@$%X#!!" Normal and healthy reaction to being told that your cholesterol is through the roof. (See also *TexMex Deprivation in Golden Agers*, Oxford University Press).

Grab Bar Device used to senior-proof one's home; often the first sign that one is capitulating to the aging process, especially if also used to dry wet support socks.

God Supreme Being in whom you believe because:

You're the first person in history to *gain* weight on chemo.

Your legs can still handle a miniskirt.

You got a surprise e-mail from an old girlfriend whom you still have in your heart.

Chest Pains Ordinary and normal response to the thought of mowing the lawn.

Your wife presenting you with a honey-do list.

"Specials of the Day" Something you ask the waiter to repeat if you're too vain to wear a hearing aid.

Valium The medicine of choice after a. ten hours with your grandchildren, or b. your ex tells you she's marrying someone half your age.

Cougar What your ex becomes after spending $20,000 of your alimony on plastic surgery and tango lessons.

Mini-bar All-purpose dispensary to help pass the time in your doctor's waiting room more enjoyably.

Senior Moment Officially defined as using a. a corkscrew to open a screw-top wine bottle, and b. a tea cozy as a yarmulke (see also additional alerts throughout).

"Outward Bound" Refers to either a great-outdoors adventure or an exceptionally satisfying bowel movement.

Biopsy What a cruel lab technician makes you wait two weeks to hear the results of.

Triple Bypass Technique used to avoid the three people to whom you owe money.

Irrational Exuberance Source of much erectile dysfunction. The most reliable cure, other than Viagra, is a visit to Lourdes.

Digestive System Internal mechanism you contact and obtain permission from before consuming two slices of double-rich chocolate cake on your sixty-first birthday.

Kvell Slang term for the profound and joyful emotion that you experience when a. someone remarks that "your new hairdo makes you look ten years younger," or b. your spouse still remembers the words to "your song."

I.Q. Test Alternate name for the Briggs-Haley Hospital-Gown Aptitude Test, which determines intelligence according to how quickly a patient, by simply following the instructions "back goes front, front goes back," can put on a hospital gown without either bursting into tears of frustration or deciding he's going home. (The record—eight minutes, fifty-two seconds—was achieved with the assistance of a kindly orderly.)

Anxiety The haunting fear, when taking Communion, that the Holy Wafer contains trans fats.

- Painful intercourse is a hot-button topic at your Jane Austen reading club.
- When asked who your doctor is, you have to reply, "For which body part?"
- Poker night topics include hot babes and colon health.
- You learn to use the computer so you can purchase discount drugs.
- Staying awake during dinner theater is your latest magic trick.
- The hair in your soup is from your nose.
- Expressing your inner child means releasing a really satisfying belch.
- Your dentist (whose children paid for Yale with the money from your root canals) tries to convince you that better teeth will attract better men.

IMPORTANT NUMBERS

82% The chances of your biopsy turning out negative if you keep your fingers crossed.

22 Number of minutes you'll cheerfully hold for an HMO rep before applying for a pistol permit.

3 to 5 years Standard prison term for passing a bad check to purchase Viagra.

106 Typical, and aerobically beneficial, heart rate while doing an in-flight pee-pee dance if the lavatory's occupied.

412 Number of pounds, by law, a person must weigh before an orderly can substitute a salad bowl for a bed pan.

4852 Number of moments you need to think when he asks, "Am I the best you've ever been with?"

8 Number of times you get up at night to urinate before deciding to sleep in the sink.

.03% Chance of controlling your bladder when pulled over for speeding in a construction zone.

1 minute, 28 seconds Time it takes to climb out of a La-Z-Boy during a heart attack.

3 minutes, 17 seconds Time it takes for an alert senior to realize the jacket he's wearing still has the hanger in it.

2 Months required to digest any potato knish purchased from a street cart with an umbrella.

52 Number of minutes the average patient spends in a doctor's waiting room before he begins to mildew.

A022477930-62088 Your HMO's secret authorization number for your next CAT scan (no contrast).

7 Number of years to subtract from your age when you're carded at a liquor store (disregard if the clerk is your son).

.000000245 of an inch How much actual enhancement to expect when you use a male-enhancement product, especially one with a disclaimer that reads, "Results are not typical."

844 Number of tears shed when you try on your old army uniform and see yourself in the mirror.

5 Number of years older using a suitcase with wheels makes you look.

Q. I want to shave a few years off my actual age. Suggestions?

A. 60 is the new 50, or, if you possess remarkable genes, 45. Hence, the answer to your question can be expressed by geriatric specialist Dr. Mel Mishkin's

Third Law of Acceptable Fibbing: NQRA = NS x $$ + TJ

HR + SIC

In which NQRA (not quite real age) equals NS (number of seconds it takes to thoroughly shuffle a pinochle deck) multiplied by $$ (amount you've spent on a chiropractor with a bad back) plus TJ (tightness of jaw line as determined by the Hochmann-McGinty Scale of Sagging Flesh), divided by HR (heart rate after vigorously mixing a salad) plus SIC (spike in cholesterol after passing out at an all-you-can-eat fish fry).

DISCLAIMER: Above does not apply if you chain smoke, are forty or more pounds overweight, or spend at least thirty-five hours a week lying in the sun.

- Religious freedom means the right to nod off during a sermon.

- You stay limber by timing the market.

- You know it's too late for a face-lift because the surgeon's incision starts above the ear and continues into the next room.

- Staring into your just-married daughter's empty closet makes you sad.

- A bong is now the sound a bell makes.

- "Fragrance for men" means WD-40.

- Your high school sweetheart now weighs more than the Buick you drove her to the prom in.

- A wobbly wheel on a shopping cart sends you over the edge.

- You prefer the term *amnesia* to *dementia*.

- You spend the month of June trying to thread a needle.
- Your psychic doubles her malpractice insurance.
- You no longer seem to be able to read without moving your lips.

- Lunch consists of oatmeal and eleven pills.

- When you finally let go of all that negative stuff, your pants fall down.

- A vision of your heirs squabbling over your estate gives you something to live for.

- A single pimple makes you feel like a teenager again.

- At your class reunion you note with satisfaction that the captain of the football team wears a hearing aid.

THINGS YOU SHOULD KNOW BY THE TIME YOU TURN 60

Never trust a thin baker.

Even if he's in your plan, avoid an allergist who has watery eyes.

There was never a General Tso.

Wearing a hospital gown doesn't make you look like a ninja.

An ultrasound is not a high-end stereo.

It's easier to give up smoking than rugelach.

It is a bad idea to frequent a nutritional counselor who accepts her co-pay in cupcakes.

How to waste time productively.

During a hospital stay, snapping your fingers doesn't make the nurse come faster.

Never frequent a medical facility with a waiting room whose magazines are sticky.

Living on the edge means:

Missing a dose of your medicine.

Using a super-sharp knife to slice a bagel in half without first putting on your glasses.

Performing at a karaoke bar, sober.

After seventy minutes, the effort required to get out of a dentist's chair requires a morphine drip.

Do not wear low-rise jeans after taking a stool softener.

Medicare doesn't pay for tattoos.

It's time to sell your G.I. Joe collection.

The recipes for:

A Merry Widow Cocktail
An "I'm Still a Bachelor" Bloody Mary
A Male-Enhancement Device Vodka Stinger

How to legally evict a 33-year-old son who won't leave home.

True self-acceptance is sunbathing in a Speedo.

Running for a bus is aerobic exercise.

Knowledge of quantum physics is helpful when trying to understand your "prescription coverage gap."

When mall walking, it's better to reach for Birkenstocks than Jimmy Choos.

"Buyer's remorse" refers to the exercise equipment, impulsively purchased from a late-night infomercial, gathering dust in your garage.

The only thing that makes time stand still is constipation.

Multitasking means a. reading e-mail while holding for the next customer service rep, and b. having acid reflux while driving a golf cart.

There is a causal connection between that glad-to-be-alive feeling of well-being and double coupons.

A romantic candlelight dinner in a dim restaurant can make thinning hair look thicker.

How to say "It's okay, we can just cuddle" without making him feel suicidal.

Never trust a brewmaster with a flat stomach.

Get off the plane if they're de-icing the wings with matches.

The chief cause of irregularity is worrying about regularity.

Never use a decorator who is straight.

REJOICE! That creaking sound you hear when you bend over to pick up loose change proves that you're still alive.

- You pull an all-nighter to study for your prostate exam.
- For Christmas you get your first defibrillator.
- You're wondering why your cardiologist now wants his co-pay *before* your stress test.
- You're booked for driving under the influence of a laxative.

- "Magical thinking" means you think you still look good in a muscle shirt.
- You become more spiritual and find a swami who takes Medicare.
- You're still sure the elevator will come faster if you press the little button fourteen times.
- You think mortality applies only to your obese neighbor with the hot dog dependence.
- Drinking responsibly means leaving enough in the bottle for a nightcap.
- The meadows where you sowed your wild oats are now shopping malls.
- You've achieved enough wisdom to know you should delete the e-mail from the Nigerian banker who is eager to send you $20 million.

60 IS THE NEW 50 IF . . .

"Performance anxiety" refers to your fear of bungee jumping.

When you take public transportation, no compassionate stranger offers you a seat.

You still look great in stilettos.

When you fly, they trust you in the emergency exit seat.

The bartender asks for ID.

You still have your wisdom teeth.

Adult education means tango lessons.

You buy your first trampoline.

You're still being dunned by your high school English teacher for that Shakespeare paper.

You still can't keep from laughing when Uncle Bill cuts one at the dinner table.

You still can't sleep with a nightlight.

You've yet to have sex in a Winnebago.

- You're excited that your grandson is nearly old enough to paint your kitchen cabinets.

- In the morning, you don't put on your socks without first checking with your back.

- RESTROOMS FOR PATRONS ONLY sign no longer applies to you.

- You refuse to let your doctor measure your height.

- Your nightly thrill is sleeping all the way through it.
- You're proud that you can still take out a flippant sales clerk with just one punch.

- Without glasses you can't tell if it's a mole or your watch.
- Your baby fat graduates to cellulite.
- You unexpectedly come home and catch your husband in bed with a heating pad.
- Dating a man half your age sounds about right.

ARE YOU A HOT SIXTY?

(Turning 60 doesn't mean you have to *be* 60. Take our scientific test to determine exactly how hot you still are.)

Your hairdresser charges extra because your hair is so thick. TRUE ____ FALSE ____

People mistake you for your daughter's sister.
TRUE ____ FALSE ____

When you wear a skimpy top, guys try to peek when you lean forward. TRUE ____ FALSE ____

You've still got the legs to wear shorts under a barbecue apron. TRUE ____ FALSE ____

You can get your tightest jeans on without lying down. TRUE ____ FALSE ____

Putting on makeup and wearing that slinky little cocktail dress still makes your husband's prostate vibrate. TRUE ____ FALSE ____

You wore out your husband (again) on your second honeymoon. TRUE ____ FALSE ____

While on jury duty, the judge came on to you.
TRUE ____ FALSE ____

So did the defendant. TRUE ____ FALSE ____
I WISH ____

Your daughter doesn't freak when you wear capri pants. TRUE ____ FALSE ____

Your granddaughter thinks your new piercing rocks.
TRUE ____ FALSE ____

Cellulite? *Moi?* TRUE ____ FALSE ____

You're getting a little bored with always hearing "Great buns!" from your gynecologist.

TRUE ____ FALSE ____

You've yet to attend a keg party where you didn't get come-hither looks from your son's best friend.

TRUE ____ FALSE ____

You refuse to wear anything but Prada sunglasses after cataract surgery. TRUE ____ FALSE ____

Your husband still playfully snaps your thong.

TRUE ____ FALSE ____

You skip your garden club meeting because you have to study for your lap dance recertification.

TRUE ____ FALSE ____

You still don't need glasses to use an ATM.

TRUE ____ FALSE ____

Your fertility doctor insists there's still hope.
TRUE ____ FALSE ____

You can still handle attending a PTA meeting bra-less. TRUE ____ FALSE ____

Scoring: Answering "true" to five or more questions makes you hot. Answering "false" to all eighteen questions is unfortunate.

- You think *Screw the little ingrates* and spend the kids' tuition on getting your bags removed and your teeth capped.
- Having your inseam measured for new track pants no longer arouses you.
- You happily add five dollars to the co-pay if your gynecologist warms the speculum.
- You care less about same-sex marriage and more about some-sex marriage.

- If you avoided all the foods you're supposed to, you'd weigh eleven pounds.

- Your first question after sex is "Was it good for me?"
- Stepping on a dime causes you to lose your balance.
- The doctor who keeps you waiting helps you fill your day.
- You seek counseling because you aren't drinking enough.

SEX AFTER 60

Until now, the problem of how to behave in the bedroom after 60 appeared unsolvable. There were few guidelines concerning how much love to make, what position best allows pleasure for the partner with a slipped disk (author's choice: back-to-back), and whether frantic grunting is a factor in deep-pore facial cleansing. Happily, our research shows that sex after 60 is pretty much the same as sex before 60, except a. the cuddling is more intense, and b. the one forbidden position mentioned on page 54 of the Iowa Book of Senior Lust (male on top, female glancing at her watch) is permissible. Because, however, the brain is the body's true sexual organ, we do caution against the use, by the female partner, of the following phrases, especially if her partner is sensitive:

"Avon calling."

"Perhaps it was counterfeit Viagra?"

"Want to buy a lottery ticket?"

"Is that all it does?"

"Your wife is on the phone."

"Can we please slow down?" (applies to sex on a gurney)

- "Thinking boldly" means ordering sweetbreads.

- He finally leaves his wife for you, because she died.

- For your partner's Valentine's Day gift you're torn between lubricating gel and itch cream.

- You ask the telemarketer what she's wearing.

- You suspect that those "specially formulated for seniors" vitamins would work just as well on a 12-year-old.

- You discover a flyer from Dial-a-Casket under your windshield wiper.
- It would be nice if you could gain height as easily as you gain weight.
- Your granddaughter is shaving her legs.
- You'd rather be water-boarded than divulge your real age.
- As your Patient of the Month price, your HMO presents you with a snow globe containing your kidney stones.
- You still have faith in humanity, but it's in T-bills.
- Your sexual philosophy becomes: "Past performance is no guarantee of future results."
- Caring about the planet makes you wonder which is greener: a hip or knee replacement.
- "Designated Baby Sitter" is the honorary title conferred upon you by your children.

HANDY EMERGENCY PHRASES

(Helpful self-explanatory expression for some typical over-60 situations)

"But I do not wish to donate bone marrow."

"Am I bleeding much?"

"Am I drooling much?" (This is often used when it's pointed out that your bingo card is wet.)

"Such a costly colon cleanse?"

"Stop, thief." (In addition to obvious situations, this can be used if you discover an orderly trying to steal your kidney.)

"Is there a doctor in the casino?"

"No, I do not wish to consolidate my credit card debt." (This is a polite way to decline the services of a telemarketer named Mike, actual name Baboo Masood Gefilte.)

"Hit my ankles with that shopping cart again and I will shove this baguette up your rectum."

"Excuse me, doctor. Why does a life insurance rep have a desk in your examining room?"

"Are those forceps clean?" (Note: This is an especially handy phrase to know if your daughter's water breaks while you and she are traveling in a third-world country.)

"That's one lovely stool." (This gets you on the good side of the other patient in your semiprivate room.)

"I'm sorry, I didn't mean to offend you." (This is the apology of choice when you come on to a particularly luscious candy striper.)

"How far is it to the border?" (This is a favorite for those whose Tijuana liposuction has gone horribly wrong.)

- Your blood tests positive for crabbiness.
- You're training yourself to use your shopping cart as a weapon.
- The new eyeglass chain around your neck miraculously makes you appear twenty years older.
- *Osteoporosis* wins you the Scrabble game.
- After conferring with a plastic surgeon, you realize that money *can* buy happiness.
- You so want to believe that green tea burns belly fat.
- Exercising willpower means resisting that Elvis compilation CD (just $19.95, plus shipping and handling).

- You turn to the obituaries and wonder, *What the hell are "unknown causes"?*

- Stage fright means that first lunch with friends after your face-lift.

- Your fortune-teller asks, "Why bother?"
- The game of shuffleboard fills you with profound depression.

- The two things you now do religiously are pray and floss.
- Your new marital aid is a motion detector.
- You're sure those tiny crow's feet make you appear more interesting.

- Your kids forbid you to shovel snow.

- You weep unashamedly the first time you catch a glimpse of yourself in cruise wear.

TRUE AGE TEST #5–YOU'RE 60 GOING ON 20 IF:

You call in sick to go kayaking.

Your parents increase your allowance.

Hot dogs are still your comfort food.

You're an egg donor.

You still run the other way when your neighbor tries to fix you up with a shriveled little guy who looks like Yasser Arafat.

Your hairline hasn't budged since high school.

You have received the President's Fitness Council "Still Most Toned Upper Arms" certificate (suitable for framing).

You pull wine corks without wrenching your back.

You associate the term *nursing home* with breast-feeding.

You're embarrassed to tell your dermatologist that the blotches on your neck are love bites.

Your parents still want to know when you're going to give them grandchildren.

Your son still can't beat you in Ping-Pong.

- Before you hit the mall, you TiVo the Weather Channel so you don't miss a tornado.

- You buy your first grab bar.

- You spend the month of July trying to climb out of your son's Porsche.

- At night you lie awake wondering, *Is my bladder half full or half empty?*
- Defensive eating includes organic bran.
- You stop using that handheld shower device for naughty things.
- You cope with empty nest syndrome by getting a parrot.
- You adopt a cat.
- You develop a supernatural ability to metabolize Imodium.
- Your urologist honors you with a coveted "Strong, Steady Stream" certificate.
- Consuming the celery in your Bloody Mary is your idea of a nutritional drink.

- Most of the men who come on to you look like your father.

- You pass on Bring Your Daughter to Work Day because she owns the company.

- What was once wild, uninhibited, four-hour sex is now a senior moment.

- Senior Moment #1: You realize you're on a blind date with someone you met thirty years ago (and he's wearing the same shirt).

- You trade in your Harley for a cat carrier.

- Lots of your friends seem to be getting married again.

- You refer to your wine cellar as a “wellness center.”

SENIOR MOMENTS

Drinking the little parasol in your mai tai.

Forgetting how to nag your spouse.

- You buy your first housecoat.
- Flannel is king.
- Senior Moment #2: You remember your password but forget what it's for.
- You stop taking it personally that you have homely grandchildren.

SENIOR MOMENT

During torrid lovemaking you want to call out his name but can't remember what it is.

- You're on your fourth puppy, your second husband, and your third yoga mat.

- After you throw yourself at a woman, she has to help you up.

- Squinting is your default position.
- Metamucil becomes a gateway drug.
- That empty seat on the bus has your name on it.

SENIOR MOMENTS

1. You don't realize you missed your exit until you see a billboard proclaiming WELCOME TO UTAH.
2. You ask the information desk at the mall where you parked your car.
3. You look down at the floor and wonder, as you hunt for your glasses, *Is that a raisin or a roach?*
4. You make the bed while your husband's still in it.
5. You try to answer correctly when your children ask you a trick question like "What day is it?"
5. You receive a "Get Well" card and wonder what's wrong with you.
6. After a long walk, you hope the dog remembers how to get home.
7. You check your name tag at your class reunion so you know how to introduce yourself.

- You hope the lighting is kind at your next speed-dating event.

- When the doctor removes the wax from your ears, he charges you by the kilo.

- The question "How much for an ounce?" refers to fresh basil.

- The way to your heart is through an angioplasty.

- At Christmas, you find a kidney in your stocking.

- You get a full body wax, and they charge extra for your eyebrows.

MORE "YOU KNOW YOU'RE 60" SENIOR MOMENTS

You order a pastrami on rye at the hardware store.

Your kindly neighbor gently points out that you're raking the leaves in your underwear.

You suddenly realize that those people living in the house with you are your children.

After carefully following a recipe for roast loin of pork with sausage stuffing, you discover you've built a bookcase.

When you try to tell someone about your dark past, you can't remember what it is.

You think S&M is a supermarket.

You tenderize the roast with fabric softener.

You walk halfway across the parking lot before noticing you didn't unbuckle your seat belt.

Your doctor explains that "turn your head and cough" is not a dance step.

You carefully try to insert a breath mint in a parking meter.

You plead with the mailman to bring you better mail.

You wonder why your personal trainer is using the litter box.

You think you really are Napoleon.

- You feel no guilt about self-medicating while waiting for the results of a CT scan.

- Sometimes, being bedridden doesn't sound like such a bad thing.

MUSIC TO YOUR EARS: NICE-TO-HEAR PHRASES THAT MAKE YOU FEEL TEN YEARS YOUNGER

"I hate you; you never seem to age."

"Have you been exercising?"

"I love women in their early fifties."

"Why don't you have any wrinkles?"

"Brow lift? Come back in ten years. Now get out of here."

"Wow! I've never had sex on a rickshaw!"

"It's benign."

"You look so majestic on that unicyle."

"Are you still a nympho?"

- Champagne for breakfast becomes a key factor in effective anger management.

- Being told, "Wow! You look terrific" makes your day, until he asks for the loan.

- You prepare for your first round-the-world cruise by learning to say "I have to go potty" in nineteen languages.

- Your eyeglasses are now called spectacles.

- Your spouse initiates sexual activity by making tea.

- Just because your name's not in the obits doesn't mean you're feeling well.

- You assault the travel agent who suggests an Elderhostel.
- You wish you hadn't spent your twenties, thirties, forties, and fifties sunbathing.

- You realize that regularity is overrated.
- You pimp your walker with whitewalls and tailfins.
- You purchase your first male-enhancement herbal supplement and discover that it smells exactly like oregano.

CONFUSING SENIOR MOMENT

When you stand up suddenly, the blood doesn't know whether to rush to your head or your feet.

- You take a swing at someone who uses the term *golden years*.
- When you purchase a movie ticket, you get the senior discount without asking for it.
- You start to believe that reincarnation makes a lot of sense.
- You finally appreciate the irony of a thoracic surgeon who also loves Cuban cigars.
- You remember when you didn't have to lock your car.
- Your contemporaries' cocktail parties include high-fiber hors d'oeuvres.

SENIOR MOMENT

You're chewing, but can't remember why.

- Peeing with a strong, steady stream becomes thrilling.
- You have reading glasses strewn throughout the house.
- You fondly recall when sex was a contact sport.
- You need to do warm-up stretches before trimming your toenails.
- Sandals with socks and a cardigan becomes your fashion statement.
- You avoid buying anything with some assembly required.
- You think trans fats are the new weapon of mass destruction.

FACE TIME WITH YOUR DOCTOR

Two questions to ask:

How green is my knee replacement?

Will you still love me if I don't get better?

- Widows of a certain age are sending you mash notes, accompanied by their homemade casseroles.

- When your frail 92-year-old mother screams, "Help, I've fallen and I can't get up," you confiscate her ice skates.

- You confront fears of aging by rethinking your lack of belief in a higher power.

- You nod at complete strangers.

- She stops trying to change you.

OFFICIAL SCALE OF RIVETING MEDICAL STORIES

Do chest pains one-up a torn ligament? You bet. Does a stab wound from an alcoholic aunt outrank high blood pressure? Of course. How often have you listened while someone natters on about their insignificant and tedious medical condition while you wonder *When do we get back to me?* You don't want pity, you want an audience. In order of fascination, these are just a few of the medical topics least likely to put your listeners to sleep and *which should*, instead, make them nod their heads with *please-tell-me-more* vigor.

Affliction	Outranks
Coronary bypass	Diabetes
Shark bite	Thyroid deficiency
Gunshot wound from jealous mistress	Constipation

Sprained ankle while skiing	Shingles
Getting dumped for a younger woman	Early-bird special food poisoning
Concussion from drag racing	Fecal incontinence
Arrhythmia due to insufficient oxygen while ascending Everest	Heartburn caused by injudicious consumption of cocktail franks
Sunstroke at clothing-optional beach	Autopsy
Motorcycle accident	Swollen prostate
Bar fight	Arthritis
Stab wound while breaking up a fight between your poker buddies	Choking on a crouton
Severe hand injury when cherry bomb prematurely exploded	Rectal itch
Dislocating shoulder while whitewater rafting the Colorado	Bunion
Anorexia	Ulcer

Abnormal heart rhythm induced by sexual demands of hot babe	Diverticulitis
Giant hangover from overindulging in the night-life in Gstaad	Parcheesi-related hernia
Falling from the crow's nest of a yacht	Exhaustion caused by three hours in a revolving door
Chapped hands from intense arm-wrestling tournament	Chapped hands from rubbing Grandma's feet
Getting slapped by humorless cocktail waitress	Weak urinary stream
Black eye from mixed martial arts session	Failure of Tucks
Trying to solve challenging Sudoku puzzle caused stress fracture	Persistent cough
Accident while riding mountain bike rendered you unconscious	Morning stiffness
Heart attack from effort of extracting hand from a Pringles can	Blood clot
African sleeping sickness	Asymmetric mole

- You wish you could disappear when you're caught putting out the trash without bothering to wear a bra.

- You find yourself with a blind date who breaks the ice by saying, "So, how do you want to be remembered?" (Probably not a keeper.)

- After an MRI, you grow paranoid when you get home and find your doctor's "call my office" message on your answering machine.

- Your ophthalmologist promotes you from 2.25 to 2.50.

- You start ordering apparel from the Home Shopping Network that contains the word *slimming*.

- You take out an order of protection against the AARP.

- You prefer the term *boo-boo* to *tumor*.

- You've been seeing your therapist for so long she Tweets you for help with her other patients.

CAN'T-FAIL PICKUP LINE USED BY OLDER MEN WHEN APPROACHING A YOUNGER WOMAN

"How would you like to be my widow?"

- Against your better judgment you order a supplement that reverses the aging process by making your pulse run backward.
- You no longer think a rotator cuff is a fashion accessory.
- You buy your first clock with jumbo digits.
- You can't understand why your date signals for the check when you pull out pictures of your grandchildren.
- When reheating a cup of coffee, you stand in front of the microwave and yell, "Come on! Come on!"

- You're beginning to doubt the aesthetic benefits of an increasingly wispy comb-over.

- You buy a fanny pack.

- You turn saving coupons into a science.

- Getting pulled over for speeding makes you feel young again.

- Your drug dealer is now your hairdresser.

- You wonder if you are going to need that five-year exemption letter from your next jury duty summons.

- Considerate friends up the font size on their e-mails to you.

- You always feel a draft.

- You accept that atonement for your sins is a nagging backache.

THINGS EVERY BABY BOOMER MUST KNOW

How to tunnel your way out of a nursing home

How to foil a debt collector

How to have sex in a limo

How to recant a deathbed confession should you get better

How to realize your full potential while lounging in a hammock

How to search Google for your childhood sweetheart

How to calculate the life expectancy of a hateful husband

How to get on a moving airplane

How to stab a surly nurse with your IV needle

How to check into a hospital under an assumed name

YOU KNOW YOU'RE 60 WHEN . . .

How to drop a persistent time-share salesman with just one punch

How to use a pillow to stifle the weird moans coming from the other patient in your semiprivate room

How to evade capture by an orderly

How to resist the temptation to pump the "claim denied" people full of lead

How to get a hot nurse to show more cleavage

How to avoid a brother-in-law who needs $10,000 to open a tanning salon

How to shake a store detective

How to lie about your age (why be a slave to your birth certificate?)

- An ill-mannered teen calls you "Pops."

- At the airport, *you're* the passenger needing special assistance.

- You develop an overwhelming curiosity about your Social Security benefits.

- You're delivering more eulogies than wedding toasts.

- Now it's *you* who's driving that slow-moving Winnebago you were always stuck behind.

- In addition to fibbing about your age, you lie about your blood pressure ("One-fifteen over seventy-three, and that's after eating a pound of salt"), thus inspiring blood-pressure envy in those half your age.

- You've read all the magazines in your doctor's waiting room—twice.

- Lately you've been wondering how your staid nurse-practitioner would look in a French maid's outfit.

- Instead of the bartender, it's your pharmacist who asks, "What'll it be, pal?"

- Instead of beer, your six-pack is now Ensure.

- Happiness is a warm catheter.

AWESOME THINGS TO DO BEFORE YOU TURN 70

Calisthenics.

Lose your virginity.

Make a video of your heirs squabbling over your estate.

Vow that there's more to look forward to than an evening of balloon sculpting at an assisted-living center.

Learn to look fabulous in a hospital gown (our hospital fashion consultant suggests accessorizing with a feather boa and pearls).

Release your inner anarchist and:

Get a piercing.
Blow .25 on a Breathalyzer.
Buy illegal fireworks.

Get Brandy, the candy striper with the sumptuous butt, to touch you in a naughty place.

Hunt down and kill the person who invented the childproof cap.

Sneak Creole jambalaya into your feeding tube.

Get beyond the second page of *Moby-Dick*.

Slaughter your own hog.

Volunteer as a bouncer in a nursing home.

Reverse your vasectomy and date someone half your age.

Toss out the seventeen shirts you're certain will be back in style any day.

Hire a guy named Mountainous Tony to collect the money your brother-in-law has owed you for twenty-two years.

Skip one annual checkup.

Rollerblade down a waterslide.

Defy the odds and breathe secondhand cigar smoke.

In your will, cut out the relative who gave you the Life Alert for Chanukah.

Get hot women to throw their underwear at you after a standout karaoke performance.

While waiting for a connecting flight, pass the time productively by getting trashed.

Learn to speed-chop vegetables without having to dial 911.

Find the courage to put on noise-canceling headphones when your wife asks, "Are you listening to me?"

Use a lash extender as a marital aid.

Close your eyes when approaching a blind curve to see how it really feels.

Chuckle audibly at the funeral of the woman who stole your ex.

Tell a beautiful woman that you want her to be the grandmother of your children.

- Without asking, the sadistic driver kneels the bus for you.

- You're convinced of the merits of single-malt scotch as a stool softener.

- You're angry that the color of your hospital ID bracelet does nothing for your eyes.

- You start waving to people.

- You no longer care about getting into a prestigious assisted-living center.

- You've earned the right to nap between each sit-up.

- Even if you stop smoking and start an exercise program, you can't possibly outlive your shirts.

- Your parents stop asking when you're going to give them grandchildren.

- You stand tall when a pretty girl walks by, as though she might actually look at you.

- You ask if your prescription bottle labels come in large print.

- The possibility of cracking a molar on a marshmallow is not remote.

- Your spouse starts helping you cut your meat.

- Your medical-appointments calendar takes up much of the space on your hard drive.

- You become a bird-watcher.

- You can recall when five cents got your letter delivered.

- You hire a full-time nurse so you can use the carpool lane.

- You often wake up at three A.M. wondering, *Is my money working hard enough for me?*

OVER-60 GUILTY PLEASURES

"Talking my thoracic surgeon into throwing in a pedicure." —Brandy, hairdresser

"Shoplifting adult-strength diapers." —Todd, lawyer

"Hacking into my blood-pressure monitor and lowering the reading so that my mistress thinks I'm healthy." —Lance, mogul

"My blog. It reveals the sordid details of our retirement community." —Tracey, Realtor

"Obtaining free drugs by trading favors with a lecherous pharmacist." —Alice, literary agent

"Sneaking a Krispy Kreme into my suppository." —Lyle, computer technician

"Watching soaps, sipping cognac, and ignoring the phone when my grandchildren call." —Lana, retired

"Getting my pool boy to apply bronzer."

—Sylvia, recently widowed

"Playing the slots in Vegas instead of buying Christmas gifts for my grandkids."

—Harold, has priorities in order

- "Wealth management" means dumping your husband for a well-heeled cardiac surgeon.
- You decide wearing cowboy boots will shave years off your age and make you as tall as you used to be.
- Any doctor's exam where you needn't remove your underwear is a good one.
- You tear a ligament playing charades.
- Your colorist convinces you to tap into your IRA to touch up your roots.

- You spend three hours in a revolving door.
- Beach reading includes Dr. Oz.
- You do your part for the energy crisis by taking afternoon naps.
- When the three widows you're dating all show up at the same time, you feign Alzheimer's.
- You no longer bother putting your convertible's top down because you have just three strands of hair to blow in the wind.
- You proudly flaunt your obscenely low PSA count on a bumper sticker.
- At the supermarket, you can now pick out the perfect honeydew.
- Since Woodstock, it's all been downhill.

- Flirting with your dental hygienist is the highlight of your month.

- You've paper-trained three dogs and two husbands.

- During an intimate candlelight dinner in a posh restaurant, your date introduces the subject of regularity.

- Your son is on his third house.

- That thigh tattoo you were so proud of has somehow wandered south, to just above your ankle.

- When friends ask you how you are, they endure a three-hour answer.

- Your screensaver is an eye chart.

- You're dating a much younger woman whose idea of a cultural afternoon is organizing her closet.

- You have a collection of pens from no fewer than ten pharmaceutical companies.

- Everyone in your doctor's waiting room looks even worse than you do.

- You still have faith in your ability get better at golf.

- Your doctor has found a direct correlation between the coronary and trying to understand a drug plan.

- Your dog is trained to find the remote.

- Gas relief has nothing to do with the price of fuel.

- Your dreams include silencing your husband's snoring with a fireplace tool.

- An ambulance with flashing lights makes you think, *There but for the grace of God . . .*

- Watching your favorite television programs takes precedence over your social life.

- Twenty-year-olds flirt with you because it either counts as a charitable deed or they're stoned.

THINGS EVERY OVER-60 MUST KNOW

How to stop a runaway wheelchair

How to hypnotize an orderly and make him your slave

How to fly-fish with your catheter

How to sneak out of a hospital

How to still look cool if you lose your balance on a moving bus

What you want to be when you grow up

- Arthritis prevents you from rolling a really good joint.

- You go to confession, but find you have less to confess.

- Your old hobby was collecting stamps; your new hobby is saving money

- You easily resist the siren's call because you can't hear it.

- When you hum "I'm in the Mood for Love" your spouse hands you the cat.

- You can hold forth, even captivate your audience, discussing the following bodily ailments: gout, shingles, anal fissure, overactive bladder, high triglycerides, anxiety, eczema, atrial flutter, bipolar disorder, constipation, cataracts, angina, idiopathic hunger, psoriasis, irritable bowel syndrome, enlarged prostate, logorrhea, teensy prostate, Crohn's disease, GERD, atherosclerosis, receding gums, envy, and corns.

- You realize life is getting shorter and move cocktail hour up to three P.M.

- You purchase your first product from Dr. Scholl's.

LET OUR CERTIFIED FINANCIAL PLANNER SHOW YOU HOW TO SPEND YOUR KIDS' INHERITANCE

Admittedly, if you have a low net worth, you have little to worry about.

A high net worth, on the other hand, can lead to problems, especially if you've decided to live forever. A few suggestions:

Yearly cruise (outside, first-class cabin—
"Sizzling South America" or
"Astonishing Antarctica") $20,000
New car every year $55,000
(What the heck—get a gas guzzler!)
Serious plastic surgery that stops
just this side of creepy. $100,000
Future plastic surgery touch-up fund. $40,000
Teeth capped, gums made youthful. $75,000
High-end entertainment center. $100,000
An amazing headstone $50,000

Or, if you prefer, a pre-Columbian, museum-quality urn	$75,000
New, unbreakable hips	$35,000
New knees, plus matching designer slacks	$25,000 (per knee, or $42,000 if there's a two-for-one sale)
Consorting with babes or studs who want you only for your money and you don't care, so long as they "consort"	$250,000
Tuition to put your boy toy or needy starlet through either Harvard or Yale Drama School	$200,000
Donating a wing so Harvard admissions will look favorably on your "protégés," despite laughable college board scores (low 100s)	$5,000,000
New Rolex so you can constantly check how long you have to live	$35,000

- Undoing a stuck zipper allows you to achieve your target heart rate.

- You learn the hard way, when it comes to herbal remedies, wrinkle removers, and memory-enhancement products, that "these statements have not been evaluated by the Food and Drug Administration."

- You're having a tawdry Internet affair.

- Your children are trying to fix you up.

- You suspect there's a causal connection between premature aging and saving string.

- On a car trip, your bladder starts whispering, "How much farther?"

- Senior Moment #3: After leaving home, do you make a panicky U-turn because you forgot your wife?

- Senior Moment #4: Have you ever canoed with the wrong end of the oar?

- Risk-taking means crossing against the light.

- You really feel your age when the technician helps you up after a CT scan.

- That special thing you have in common with your new lover is matching scooters.

- You have to PhotoShop your passport picture.

- "Healthy choice" means reducing your cheesecake intake.

- You look up *patriarch* in the dictionary.

- That tight feeling in your chest makes you wonder whether to call a doctor or a mortician.

- You get your first "Get Well" E-card.

- Sinatra singing "My Way" reminds you of how you like your eggs.

- You spend your grandson's college tuition fund on new hips.

- Your doctor, your dentist, and the president of the United States are all younger than you.

- You buy a lava lamp at a yard sale.

- Your fertility doctor stops returning your calls.

- You enthusiastically endorse the health effects of red wine, but not soy.

- After an afternoon of pulling weeds, you high-five yourself when you're able to stand erect without leaning on the cat.

- You're old enough to have lived the songs of your youth.

- You ask the pharmacist if your co-pay is his "opening offer."

- At swingers' parties, instead of a date, you bring a casserole.

- Your carpal tunnel syndrome is caused by downloading porn.

- Senior Moment #5: You easily find your glasses but forget what you wanted to read.

- The rate at which you lose hair and gain weight accelerates.

- All the things you thought were funny about being 60 aren't.

ABOUT THE AUTHOR

Richard Smith, the writer in residence, has over 1,200,026 books in print. He has written humor and essays for several major publications and one minor. He likes hiking, camping, fine dining, concerts, and agriculture.